POST PANDEMIC SOCIETY

Unmasking the New Mormal

Geoffrey Zachary

CONTENTS

Post-Pandemic Society: Unmasking the New Normal"

Introduction

In the wake of the global COVID-19 pandemic, the world has undergone a profound transformation.
Our daily lives, social interactions, and the very fabric of society have been reshaped in unprecedented ways.
As we emerge from the crisis, it is crucial to navigate and understand the dynamics of the new normal that awaits us.

The post-pandemic society represents a significant milestone in human history.
It is a time of reflection, adaptation, and reimagining.
We have witnessed the resilience and strength of communities, the dedication of healthcare workers, and the power of scientific advancements.
Now, as we step into this new chapter, we have an opportunity to build a better future.

We aim to unmask the complexities of the new normal and provide insights into the key areas that have been transformed by the pandemic.
From health and wellness to education, work, and social interactions, every aspect of our lives has been profoundly impacted.
It is essential to understand the challenges and opportunities that lie ahead as we navigate this uncharted territory.

The new normal is not a fixed destination but an ongoing process of adaptation and growth.
It is a state of continuous change and evolution as we learn to coexist with the virus, implement preventive measures, and embrace new ways of living.
Understanding the key characteristics of the new normal will help

us navigate the challenges and harness the opportunities that arise.

First and foremost, the new normal emphasises the importance of health and safety.
We have become more vigilant about personal hygiene, social distancing, and the need to protect the most vulnerable among us. Health and wellness have taken centre stage, with a heightened focus on mental health, resilience, and self-care.

Secondly, the new normal is defined by digital transformation.
The pandemic has accelerated the adoption of technology, transforming the way we work, learn, communicate, and access services.
From remote work arrangements to online education and telemedicine, technology has become an integral part of our daily lives, offering convenience and connectivity.

Another key aspect of the new normal is the re-evaluation of our priorities and values.
The pandemic has prompted introspection and a reassessment of what truly matters.
People are seeking more meaningful connections, valuing relationships, and prioritizing their well-being.
There is a growing recognition of the need for sustainable practices and a focus on building a greener, more resilient future.

As we embark on this journey through the post-pandemic society, it is crucial to embrace empathy, compassion, and resilience.
We must adapt to the changes around us, support one another, and work collectively to rebuild and thrive.
The challenges may be significant, but so are the opportunities for growth, innovation, and positive transformation.

We chart a course to examine the various facets of the new normal, exploring topics such as health, education, work, social interactions, governance, and more.
Through research, insights, and real-life examples, we aim to

provide a comprehensive understanding of the post-pandemic society and empower readers to navigate and thrive in this evolving landscape.

CHAPTER 1: THE PRE-PANDEMIC ERA: REFLECTING ON LIFE BEFORE THE PANDEMIC AND THE WORLD IN IGNORANCE

In the pre-pandemic era, our lives were characterized by a sense of complacency and limited preparedness for a crisis of such magnitude. Infectious diseases and global health crises were distant concerns, dismissed as unlikely occurrences. We lived in a world where the threat of a pandemic was shrouded in scepticism, and warnings from experts were met with scepticism or simply ignored.

During this time, our interconnectedness and advances in modern medicine fostered a false sense of invincibility. Outbreaks like SARS and H1N1 served as warning signs, but they were contained relatively quickly, leading to a belief that we were immune to the devastating effects of a pandemic. Our systems for global health surveillance and response were underfunded and undervalued, and we were ill-prepared to handle a crisis of such magnitude.

One real-life example that highlights our complacency is the 2009 H1N1 influenza pandemic. Despite the initial severity of the outbreak, it was not met with the same level of urgency and global cooperation as the COVID-19 pandemic. The response to H1N1 was relatively swift, but it highlighted gaps in our preparedness and response mechanisms. Lessons from the H1N1 pandemic were not fully internalized, and the world slipped back into a state of unpreparedness.

The consequences of our collective ignorance became painfully apparent when the COVID-19 pandemic struck. Our infrastructure for global health surveillance and response was stretched to its limits, and our stockpiles of essential medical supplies proved insufficient. The rapid development and production of vaccines and therapeutics on a large scale became an unprecedented challenge. The shortcomings of our systems and protocols were exposed, revealing the need for a more robust and prepared approach to global health security.

Real-life examples further illustrate the consequences of our unpreparedness. The delayed response to the pandemic in some countries led to overwhelmed healthcare systems, high mortality rates, and significant economic disruptions. For instance, the lack of early testing and containment measures in several countries contributed to the rapid spread of the virus and resulted in a surge in cases and deaths. On the other hand, countries that had invested in pandemic preparedness, such as South Korea and Taiwan, were able to mount effective responses, quickly implementing testing, contact tracing, and containment measures.

Reflecting on the pre-pandemic era allows us to understand the stark contrast between then and now. It serves as a reminder of the transformative impact the pandemic has had on our lives and the world at large. The lessons learned from this period of ignorance and complacency have paved the way for a deeper understanding of the importance of global cooperation, preparedness, and investment in public health infrastructure.

Moving forward, it is crucial to apply the lessons learned from the pre-pandemic era and real-life examples to shape a more resilient and prepared future. By acknowledging our past mistakes and taking proactive measures, we can build stronger healthcare systems, enhance global collaboration, and invest in early detection and response capabilities. Through introspection and analysis, we can forge a path towards a more resilient and prepared post-pandemic society that is better equipped to handle future challenges.

CHAPTER 2: THE GLOBAL IMPACT OF THE PANDEMIC: UNLEASHING THE INVISIBLE ENEMY AND A WORLD TRANSFORMED

The COVID-19 pandemic has had a profound and far-reaching impact on a global scale, leaving no region untouched by its rapid transmission and devastating consequences. This chapter delves into the comprehensive exploration of the profound impact unleashed by this invisible adversary, as well as the transformative changes it has brought about in our world.

The initial shock and disbelief reverberated across nations as healthcare systems were strained under the weight of rising cases and lives were tragically lost. The pandemic acted as a wake-up call, jolting us into realizing our vulnerability and the urgent necessity for global collaboration to combat this shared threat.

The pandemic swiftly infiltrated every nation and community, demonstrating the interconnectedness of our global society and the universal nature of this crisis. Borders became mere lines on a map as the virus spread relentlessly, underscoring the need for collective action and solidarity.

This global crisis has acted as a catalyst for transformative changes across various sectors of society. It shattered long-held assumptions and upended traditional practices, forcing us to reimagine the very fabric of our existence. The world of work witnessed a seismic shift as remote work and digital transformation became the new norm, allowing businesses and industries to adapt and safeguard their survival. Education underwent a revolution, with virtual classrooms and online learning platforms becoming essential tools for students worldwide. Social connections migrated to digital platforms, bridging the physical divide through virtual gatherings, video calls, and social media interactions.

However, the pandemic also laid bare the pre-existing fault lines of social and economic inequality. Vulnerable communities, already marginalized, bore the brunt of the impact, amplifying the chasm of wealth disparity. This crisis highlighted the systemic inequities that plagued our societies, demanding urgent attention and redress. In response, calls for inclusivity, equitable policies, and meaningful social reforms grew louder, aiming to shape a fairer and more just future.

Amidst the challenges, the pandemic unveiled the indomitable spirit of humanity. Communities rallied together, displaying resilience and solidarity in the face of adversity. Frontline workers, selflessly sacrificing their well-being, demonstrated unwavering dedication in caring for the sick and vulnerable. Countless acts of kindness and innovation flourished, showcasing the creative ways individuals supported and uplifted one another during these trying times.

Real-life examples further illustrate the impact of the pandemic and the strength of human resilience. Communities organized food drives to support those facing economic hardships. Artists and musicians held virtual concerts to uplift spirits and provide a sense of connection. Companies pivoted their production lines to manufacture personal protective equipment for frontline workers. These examples demonstrate the power of compassion, unity, and collective action in times of crisis.

"The Global Impact of the Pandemic" offers a panoramic view of the far-reaching effects of this unprecedented crisis. It serves as a poignant reminder that no region or population was left untouched, uniting us in our shared experiences and the collective quest to navigate the intricacies of the new normal. As we bear witness to the ongoing transformation of our world, it becomes our shared responsibility to adapt, shape, and construct a future that embodies resilience, compassion, and sustainability. Together, we have the power to build a world that is better prepared, more inclusive, and united in the face of future challenges.

CHAPTER 3: NAVIGATING UNCERTAINTY: ADAPTING TO RAPID CHANGE AND EMBRACING RESILIENCE

The post-pandemic era has ushered in a period of unprecedented change and uncertainty.
As societies and individuals navigate this uncharted territory, it becomes crucial to understand the challenges and develop strategies to thrive in this rapidly evolving world. And so, we must explore the multifaceted aspects of navigating uncertainty, including adaptability, resilience, and the importance of mental and emotional well-being.

The pandemic forced us to confront our vulnerabilities and reimagine our ways of living and working. Individuals and organizations have had to adapt swiftly to the new normal, embracing innovative approaches and technologies to ensure their survival and success. Remote work, virtual collaborations, and flexible business models have become essential components of this adaptation. According to a survey conducted by Gartner, 82% of company leaders plan to allow employees to work remotely at least some of the time, even after the pandemic subsides.

However, adapting to rapid change can take a toll on our mental and emotional well-being. Uncertainty, fear, and stress have become prevalent in our lives. Therefore, it is crucial to prioritize mental health and resilience. Research has shown that practising mindfulness and self-care techniques can help alleviate stress and improve mental well-being.
Additionally, seeking support from friends, family, and mental health professionals is vital in navigating these challenging times.

Resilience, the ability to bounce back and thrive in the face of adversity, has emerged as a critical trait in the post-pandemic world. It encompasses adaptability, optimism, and problem-solving skills. A study published in the Journal of Personality and Social Psychology found that individuals with higher levels of resilience were better equipped to handle uncertainty and experienced greater psychological well-being. Building resilience requires cultivating positive thinking, nurturing strong relationships, and developing coping mechanisms to manage stress and setbacks effectively.

Throughout history, stories of resilience have inspired and motivated individuals and communities. From healthcare workers on the frontlines risking their lives to entrepreneurs reinventing their businesses, these stories showcase the power of human resilience. For instance, during the pandemic, many small businesses pivoted their operations to meet the changing demands, such as restaurants offering takeout and delivery services and gyms providing virtual fitness classes.
These examples demonstrate the adaptive spirit and creativity needed to thrive in uncertain times.

Uncertainty also presents opportunities for growth and transformation. The post-pandemic world provides a chance to reimagine our lives and societies, with a renewed focus on sustainability and equity. Innovations in technology, healthcare, and social systems have the potential to shape a more resilient and inclusive future. Collaboration between individuals, organizations, and governments is essential to drive these changes and ensure a more sustainable and equitable world for future generations.

Navigating uncertainty requires fostering a sense of hope and optimism. Research has shown that maintaining a positive mindset and a sense of purpose can enhance overall well-being and resilience. Finding meaning in our actions and embracing change as an opportunity for personal and collective growth can help us navigate uncertainties with confidence and resilience.

Adapting to Rapid Change and Embracing Resilience serves as a comprehensive guide for individuals and communities seeking to adapt and thrive in the post-pandemic world. By understanding the challenges of rapid change, embracing resilience, and prioritizing mental well-being, we can navigate uncertainty with confidence and build a future filled with opportunities for growth and renewal.

CHAPTER 4: REINVENTING WORK AND EDUCATION

The post-pandemic society has witnessed a profound transformation in the way we work and learn. The rise of remote work and online learning has reshaped our professional and educational landscapes, requiring us to redefine the workplace and classroom. In this chapter, we will explore these shifts in detail, examining their benefits, challenges, and the technological advancements that have facilitated this transformation.

Remote work has emerged as a viable option for organizations, enabling employees to work from the comfort of their homes or any location outside the traditional office setting. This shift has brought numerous advantages. It offers increased flexibility, allowing individuals to balance work and personal commitments more effectively. Commuting time is reduced, leading to improved work-life balance and reduced carbon emissions. Additionally, remote work opens opportunities for businesses to tap into a global talent pool, as geographical barriers are no longer limitations. However, it also presents challenges. Maintaining effective communication and collaboration in virtual settings can be demanding, requiring the use of video conferencing tools, project management software, and other digital platforms. Organizations must also address concerns related to data security and employee well-being.

Similarly, the education sector has embraced online learning to ensure continuity in education during times of disruption. Online platforms and learning management systems have enabled students to engage in remote learning, access educational resources and interact with instructors and peers virtually. This approach offers flexibility, personalized learning experiences, and increased accessibility, breaking down geographical barriers and providing education to those who may have limited access otherwise. However, it also poses challenges, such as the need for reliable internet connectivity and access to digital devices. It requires educators to adapt their teaching methods to the virtual environment and find innovative ways to foster student engagement and social interaction.

Technological advancements have played a pivotal role in enabling remote work and online learning. Video conferencing platforms like Zoom, Microsoft Teams, and Google Meet have become essential tools for virtual meetings and collaboration. Learning management systems such as Canvas, Moodle, and Blackboard provide a centralized platform for course materials, assignments, and communication. Cloud storage and file-sharing services facilitate seamless access to documents and resources from anywhere. The integration of artificial intelligence and virtual reality technologies holds promise for further enhancing the remote work and learning experience.

The redefinition of the workplace and classroom extends beyond virtual settings. Physical spaces must adapt to meet the changing needs and priorities of individuals and organizations. The concept of hybrid work has gained traction, allowing employees to work from both physical and remote locations. This model offers the advantages of in-person collaboration and social interaction while preserving the flexibility and autonomy of remote work. Employers are exploring innovative approaches to office design, incorporating flexible seating arrangements, collaborative spaces, and enhanced sanitation measures to ensure employee safety and well-being.

In education, a blended learning approach has emerged, combining online and in-person instruction. This model provides the benefits of personalized learning experiences and increased accessibility while recognizing the importance of face-to-face interactions for social development and hands-on learning. Schools and universities are reimagining their physical spaces, implementing safety measures, and creating environments conducive to both virtual and in-person learning.

Reinventing Work and Education explores the multifaceted impact of the post-pandemic society on our professional and educational spheres.

By embracing remote work, online learning, and reimagining physical spaces, we can create more flexible, inclusive, and innovative work and education systems. Technology continues to play a pivotal role in enabling these transformations, ensuring connectivity, collaboration, and access to resources.

As we navigate this new landscape, it is crucial to strike a balance between the advantages of remote work and online learning and the need for social interaction, collaboration, and human connection in both the workplace and the classroom.

CHAPTER 5: HEALTH AND WELLNESS IN THE NEW NORMAL: PRIORITIZING MENTAL AND PHYSICAL WELL-BEING AND THE EVOLUTION OF HEALTHCARE SYSTEMS

The COVID-19 pandemic has not only had a profound impact on our physical health but has also taken a toll on our mental well-being. As we navigate the new normal, it is essential to prioritize our mental and physical health. In this chapter, we will explore the importance of maintaining overall well-being and the evolution of healthcare systems to meet the challenges of the post-pandemic world.

The pandemic has highlighted the significance of self-care and mental resilience. The prolonged periods of uncertainty, social isolation, and anxiety have affected individuals' mental health. Therefore, it is crucial to develop strategies for maintaining good mental well-being. Practices such as mindfulness, meditation, and engaging in stress-reducing activities can help manage anxiety and promote mental wellness. Additionally, seeking support networks, whether through friends, family, or mental health professionals, is essential for addressing mental health challenges.

Furthermore, we will emphasize the importance of prioritizing physical health. Regular exercise, a balanced diet, and preventive healthcare measures are key components of a healthy lifestyle. The pandemic has served as a wake-up call, reminding us of the vulnerabilities of our health systems and the need for individual responsibility in taking charge of our well-being. Engaging in physical activities, maintaining a nutritious diet, and following preventive measures such as vaccinations and regular health screenings are crucial for promoting and safeguarding our physical health.

The COVID-19 pandemic has accelerated the adoption of telemedicine and remote healthcare services. These innovations have played a vital role in ensuring continued access to healthcare while minimizing the risk of transmission. Virtual doctor visits, remote monitoring of vital signs, and the use of wearable devices for tracking health metrics have become integral parts of healthcare delivery. These technologies have not only improved access to healthcare but have also facilitated early detection and intervention, leading to better health outcomes.

However, it is important to address the challenges associated with the digital divide to ensure equitable access to healthcare technology. Efforts should be made to bridge the gap and provide access to telemedicine services and digital health tools to underserved populations. By doing so, we can ensure that everyone has equal opportunities to benefit from the advancements in healthcare technology.

The pandemic has also highlighted the importance of collaboration and information sharing among healthcare professionals. Data analytics, artificial intelligence, and telehealth platforms have played a crucial role in enhancing communication and collaboration within the healthcare industry. These technologies have facilitated real-time data analysis, predictive modelling, and decision support systems, enabling healthcare providers to deliver more efficient and effective care.

Moreover, the pandemic has prompted a re-evaluation of healthcare policies and infrastructure. It has revealed the need for resilient healthcare systems that can effectively respond to crises and ensure the provision of essential healthcare services. This includes strengthening healthcare workforce capacity, improving healthcare infrastructure, and implementing robust supply chain management systems to ensure the availability of essential medical supplies and equipment.

Health and Wellness in the New Normal underscore the importance of prioritizing mental and physical well-being in the post-pandemic society. It highlights the transformative changes in healthcare systems, including the adoption of telemedicine, the use of digital health tools, and the emphasis on preventive care. By recognizing the interconnectedness of mind and body, and by leveraging advancements in healthcare technology, we can build a society that places health and wellness at the forefront. This involves fostering a holistic approach to healthcare, promoting mental resilience, and ensuring equitable access to healthcare services and resources. Through collective efforts, we can navigate the new normal with resilience and build a healthier future for all.

CHAPTER 6: TECHNOLOGY AS A CATALYST: ACCELERATING DIGITAL TRANSFORMATION AND THE POWER OF INNOVATION

The COVID-19 pandemic has acted as a powerful catalyst, accelerating the pace of digital transformation, and unleashing the full potential of technology in the post-pandemic society. In this chapter, we will explore the profound impact of technology as a catalyst for change and innovation, revolutionizing various aspects of our lives.

The pandemic has compelled organizations, industries, and individuals to swiftly adapt to the digital landscape. Remote work has become the new norm, with businesses leveraging collaboration tools and video conferencing platforms to ensure seamless communication and productivity. According to a survey by the World Economic Forum, 98% of people believe remote work will continue even after the pandemic. This shift has not only demonstrated the viability of remote work but has also highlighted its numerous advantages, including cost savings, increased flexibility, and reduced carbon footprint.

Digitalization has transformed the way we connect, collaborate, and conduct business. Virtual meetings and teleconferencing have replaced traditional face-to-face interactions, allowing for global communication and borderless collaboration. E-commerce has experienced unprecedented growth, with online shopping becoming a lifeline for consumers and businesses alike. In 2020, global e-commerce sales reached a staggering $4.28 trillion, according to Statista. This surge in online transactions has not only reshaped the retail landscape but has also led to innovations in last-mile delivery, supply chain management, and customer engagement.

The accelerated adoption of technology has not been without its challenges. The digital divide has become more evident, with marginalized communities lacking access to reliable internet connectivity and essential digital tools. Bridging this gap is crucial to ensure equitable access to opportunities in the digital age. Governments, organizations, and tech companies are investing in initiatives to expand internet access, provide digital literacy training, and distribute devices to underserved communities. Closing the digital divide is a critical step towards building an inclusive society in the post-pandemic world.

In times of crisis, innovation becomes a necessity. The pandemic has spurred remarkable innovations in healthcare, education, and beyond. Telehealth services have gained prominence, enabling remote consultations and healthcare monitoring, reducing the strain on healthcare systems, and minimizing the risk of virus transmission. Artificial intelligence and data analytics have played a pivotal role in tracking and predicting the spread of the virus, supporting decision-making processes, and accelerating vaccine development. The unprecedented development and rollout of COVID-19 vaccines have demonstrated the power of scientific innovation and collaboration in addressing global health crises.

Furthermore, the pandemic has highlighted the importance of collaboration and information sharing. Public-private partnerships have played a crucial role in accelerating technological advancements and addressing societal challenges. Governments, research institutions, and industry leaders have come together to foster innovation ecosystems, providing funding, resources, and support for start-ups and entrepreneurs. This collaborative approach has paved the way for breakthrough innovations in renewable energy, smart cities, sustainable agriculture, and more.

Technology as a Catalyst explores the transformative role of technology and innovation in reshaping the new normal. As we navigate the digital landscape, it is imperative to address ethical considerations, data privacy, and cybersecurity. Embracing digital transformation while upholding strong ethical frameworks will enable us to harness the full potential of technology for the betterment of society.

By leveraging technology as a catalyst for change, we can create a future that is not only digitally advanced but also inclusive, sustainable, and resilient. Embracing innovation, bridging the digital divide, and fostering collaboration will propel us towards a post-pandemic society where technology serves as a powerful tool for positive transformation.

CHAPTER 7: ECONOMIC RECOVERY AND SUSTAINABILITY: REBUILDING FINANCIAL SYSTEMS AND BALANCING GROWTH WITH ENVIRONMENTAL RESPONSIBILITY

The COVID-19 pandemic has had a far-reaching impact on global economies, necessitating a focused effort to rebuild financial systems and promote sustainable economic recovery. In this chapter, we will explore the strategies and measures required to navigate the path towards recovery while prioritizing environmental responsibility.

The pandemic has exposed vulnerabilities in financial systems worldwide, triggering a need for resilience and adaptability. Governments, central banks, and financial institutions have implemented various measures to stabilize economies and restore confidence. For instance, many countries introduced stimulus packages to support businesses and individuals impacted by the crisis. The International Monetary Fund (IMF) estimated that governments globally provided financial support amounting to over $12 trillion to mitigate the economic impact of the pandemic.

Moreover, the pandemic has underscored the importance of inclusive economic growth and addressing income inequality. It has revealed the disproportionate impact of crises on marginalized communities and highlighted the need for targeted support. Governments and organizations have focused on creating policies and programs to promote inclusive recovery, such as providing financial assistance to vulnerable populations, investing in skills development, and fostering entrepreneurship opportunities.

Financial literacy has emerged as a crucial component of post-pandemic economic recovery. Enhancing financial literacy empowers individuals to make informed decisions, manage their finances effectively, and access financial services. Governments and organizations have implemented initiatives to promote financial literacy, including educational campaigns, workshops, and digital tools. According to the Organization for Economic Cooperation and Development (OECD), promoting financial literacy contributes to greater financial inclusion and overall economic stability.

As we rebuild our economies, it is imperative to address sustainability and environmental responsibility. The pandemic has highlighted the interconnectedness between human well-being and the health of the planet. To ensure a more resilient and sustainable future, we must balance economic growth with environmental considerations.

The concept of a green recovery has gained traction globally.

A green recovery focuses on investment in environmentally friendly initiatives and sustainable practices. Governments and businesses have prioritized investments in renewable energy sources, such as solar and wind power, to reduce dependence on fossil fuels and mitigate climate change. The International Renewable Energy Agency (IREA) reported that the renewable energy sector employed over 11 million people worldwide in 2020, demonstrating the potential for job creation in the transition to a greener economy.

Additionally, promoting a circular economy is crucial for sustainable economic recovery. A circular economy aims to minimize waste, maximize resource efficiency, and promote recycling and reuse. By shifting from a linear "take-make-dispose" model to a circular one, we can reduce environmental impact and create economic opportunities. Organizations are implementing circular economy practices, such as product redesign, resource recovery, and extended producer responsibility, to drive sustainability and cost savings.

Furthermore, sustainable business models are emerging as key drivers of economic recovery and environmental stewardship. Businesses are increasingly integrating sustainability into their core strategies, recognizing that responsible practices can enhance their reputation, attract customers, and generate long-term value. Sustainable business models include initiatives like carbon offset programs, supply chain transparency, and ethical sourcing. The Global Reporting Initiative (GRI) provides frameworks for organizations to measure and report their sustainability performance, promoting accountability and transparency.

Economic Recovery and Sustainability emphasize the need to rebuild financial systems while prioritizing environmental responsibility. By embracing inclusive growth, enhancing financial literacy, and promoting sustainable practices, we can forge a resilient and environmentally conscious future. Balancing economic growth with environmental stewardship is essential for achieving sustainable development goals and ensuring the well-being of present and future generations.

CHAPTER 8: THE SOCIAL IMPACT OF THE PANDEMIC: ADDRESSING INEQUALITY AND SOCIAL JUSTICE ISSUES AND STRENGTHENING COMMUNITY BONDS

The COVID-19 pandemic has not only been a health crisis but has also laid bare the deep-rooted inequalities and social justice issues that persist in our societies. In this chapter, we will delve into the far-reaching social impact of the pandemic and explore strategies for addressing inequality and promoting social justice in the post-pandemic era.

One of the stark realities that the pandemic has brought to light is the disproportionate impact on vulnerable populations. Marginalized communities, including low-income individuals, racial and ethnic minorities, and people with disabilities, have borne the brunt of the pandemic's consequences. They face higher rates of infection, limited access to healthcare services, and economic instability. Addressing these disparities requires a multifaceted approach that considers the social determinants of health and works towards creating equitable conditions for all.

Healthcare inequality has been a significant concern during the pandemic. Disparities in access to quality healthcare have resulted in disproportionate outcomes for certain communities. For example, communities of colour in the United States have experienced higher COVID-19 infection and mortality rates compared to their white counterparts. Recognizing these disparities is crucial in developing targeted interventions and policies to ensure equal access to healthcare services, promote health equity, and reduce health disparities.

Education is another area profoundly affected by the pandemic, with the shift to remote learning highlighting existing educational inequalities. Students from low-income backgrounds or lacking access to technology and internet connectivity have faced significant challenges in accessing quality education. Efforts must be made to bridge the digital divide, provide necessary resources to students in need, and ensure that all learners have an equal opportunity to succeed academically.

The pandemic has also exacerbated income inequality, as many individuals and families have experienced job loss, reduced work hours, or financial instability. This has led to increased food insecurity, housing instability, and limited access to essential resources. Social safety nets, welfare programs, and inclusive policies are essential in supporting those most affected by the pandemic, ensuring that basic needs are met and enabling individuals and families to weather the economic storm.

Beyond addressing immediate needs, the pandemic has highlighted the need for long-term structural changes to promote social justice. This includes reforming criminal justice systems, combating systemic racism, and ensuring equal opportunities for all. It requires challenging and dismantling discriminatory practices and policies that perpetuate inequality.

While the pandemic has presented immense challenges, it has also underscored the power of community and the strength that can be derived from collective action. Communities have rallied together to support vulnerable individuals and families, mobilizing resources, and providing mutual aid. These acts of solidarity have strengthened community bonds and showcased the resilience and compassion that exist within our societies.

Building on this spirit of community engagement, it is crucial to foster inclusive and participatory decision-making processes that amplify marginalized voices. By involving diverse perspectives in policy discussions and implementation, we can create solutions that address the root causes of inequality and promote social justice.

Furthermore, investments in community infrastructure and social services are vital in building resilient communities. This includes affordable housing initiatives, accessible healthcare centres, community centres, and educational programs that empower individuals and facilitate social mobility.

Addressing inequality and promoting social justice requires long-term commitment and systemic change. The pandemic has presented an opportunity to confront these issues head-on and reimagine a society that is fair, inclusive, and equitable for all. By prioritizing the needs of marginalized populations, strengthening community bonds, and advocating for transformative policies, we can work towards building a post-pandemic society that upholds the principles of justice and equality. This collective effort will not only help us recover from the impact of the pandemic but also create a more resilient and just future for generations to come.

CHAPTER 9: RETHINKING TRAVEL AND TOURISM: A NEW ERA FOR TRAVEL AND SUSTAINABLE TOURISM PRACTICES

The COVID-19 pandemic has had a profound and lasting impact on the travel and tourism industry, fundamentally reshaping the way we explore and experience the world. In this chapter, we will delve into the transformation of travel in the post-pandemic era and explore the opportunities it presents for reimagining our approach to tourism.

The pandemic has necessitated new health and safety measures, with stringent protocols put in place to protect travellers and destinations alike. We have witnessed the widespread adoption of enhanced sanitation practices, social distancing guidelines, and travel restrictions. These measures have been crucial in mitigating the spread of the virus and rebuilding trust in the travel industry.

Technology has played a pivotal role in enabling contactless travel experiences. Digital health passports and mobile applications have emerged as valuable tools for verifying vaccination and testing records, providing a seamless and secure way for travellers to navigate entry requirements. Touchless check-ins, biometric scanning, and automated processes have become the new norm, reducing physical contact, and enhancing safety.

The pandemic has also accelerated the emergence of new travel trends and behaviours. Remote work and digital nomadism have gained momentum as individuals seek flexibility and the ability to work from anywhere. This shift has prompted destinations to adapt and cater to this growing segment of travellers, offering long-term stay options, co-working spaces, and amenities that support remote work.

Moreover, there is a growing recognition of the importance of adopting a more mindful and sustainable approach to travel. The concept of "slow travel" has gained prominence, encouraging travellers to immerse themselves in local cultures, support local economies, and minimize their environmental footprint. Travellers are seeking meaningful and authentic experiences, focusing on cultural exchange, community engagement, and responsible tourism practices.

Sustainable tourism initiatives are key to shaping a more responsible and resilient tourism industry. Conservation efforts, such as protecting fragile ecosystems and wildlife, have gained momentum, with travellers actively participating in eco-friendly activities and supporting conservation projects. Community-based tourism initiatives empower local communities by involving them in the tourism value chain, ensuring equitable distribution of economic benefits and fostering cultural preservation.

The post-pandemic era presents an opportunity to recalibrate tourism practices with a renewed emphasis on sustainability. By embracing sustainable tourism principles, destinations can promote economic development, preserve natural and cultural heritage, and enhance the well-being of local communities. This includes investing in infrastructure that minimizes environmental impact, supporting sustainable transportation options, and implementing responsible waste management practices.

Rethinking Travel and Tourism invites readers to reimagine the future of travel and explore sustainable practices that can shape a more responsible and resilient tourism industry. Through innovation, collaboration, and conscious decision-making, we can rebuild the travel sector in a way that balances economic growth with environmental and social well-being. By prioritizing sustainability and embracing the transformative power of travel, we can create a world where exploration and preservation go hand in hand.

CHAPTER 10: RESHAPING ENTERTAINMENT AND CULTURE: VIRTUAL EXPERIENCES AND DIGITAL ENTERTAINMENT REDEFINING ART AND EXPRESSION

The COVID-19 pandemic has transformed the landscape of entertainment and culture, giving rise to virtual experiences and digital entertainment that redefine how we engage with art and expression. In this chapter, we will explore the profound impact of these shifts and highlight real-life examples that demonstrate the transformative power of technology in the post-pandemic society.

Digital art, online galleries, and virtual exhibitions have revolutionized the art world, allowing artists to showcase their work to a global audience. For instance, the Museum of Modern Art (MoMA) in New York launched "Virtual Views," an online platform that offers immersive experiences of their exhibitions, including 360-degree views and audio guides. This initiative has enabled art enthusiasts from around the world to engage with renowned artworks and explore the museum's collections from the comfort of their homes.

The pandemic has also accelerated the digital transformation of traditional forms of entertainment. The theatre industry, for example, has embraced digital platforms to bring performances to audiences virtually. The National Theatre in London introduced "National Theatre at Home," a streaming service that offers access to their productions, including acclaimed plays like "Frankenstein" and "One Man, Two Guvnors." This initiative has allowed people worldwide to enjoy live theatre performances and support the arts during a time of physical distancing.

Furthermore, the music industry has adapted to the new normal by organizing virtual concerts and live-streaming events. Artists such as Billie Eilish and BTS have captivated audiences with their online performances, reaching millions of fans globally. These virtual concerts have not only provided a sense of connection and entertainment but have also created unique opportunities for artists to experiment with innovative visual effects and stage designs.

The role of art in fostering dialogue, resilience, and healing during times of crisis cannot be overstated. Artists have responded to the challenges posed by the pandemic by using their creativity to inspire and uplift others. For example, the "Songs of Comfort" initiative, initiated by cellist Yo-Yo Ma, encouraged musicians worldwide to share performances from their homes, spreading messages of hope and unity. Through these musical expressions, artists have brought solace to individuals grappling with the emotional toll of the pandemic.

Preserving and supporting cultural institutions and local artistic communities is essential for the continued growth and vitality of the arts. The pandemic has highlighted the vulnerability of these sectors, prompting initiatives to protect and promote cultural heritage. UNESCO's #ShareCulture campaign, for instance, encourages individuals to share their favourite cultural sites and heritage landmarks online, raising awareness about the importance of preserving these treasures for future generations.

Virtual experiences and digital entertainment have expanded the possibilities for audience engagement. Online gaming has emerged as a platform for social interaction, enabling players to connect and collaborate in virtual worlds. Games like "Animal Crossing: New Horizons" and "Fortnite" have hosted virtual concerts and events, providing a unique and interactive entertainment experience for millions of players.

In conclusion, the COVID-19 pandemic has spurred the emergence of virtual experiences and digital entertainment, reshaping the entertainment and cultural industries. Through real-life examples, we have witnessed the power of technology to connect people, promote artistic expression, and preserve cultural heritage. By embracing these innovations, supporting artists and cultural institutions, and nurturing creativity, we can foster a vibrant and inclusive artistic landscape in the post-pandemic society.

CHAPTER 11: REBUILDING TRUST IN INSTITUTIONS: RESTORING CONFIDENCE IN GOVERNMENT AND INSTITUTIONS AND STRENGTHENING TRANSPARENCY AND ACCOUNTABILITY

The COVID-19 pandemic has exposed vulnerabilities in our systems and institutions, challenging the trust and confidence placed in them. In this chapter, we will explore the crucial task of rebuilding trust in the post-pandemic society by focusing on transparency, accountability, and inclusive decision-making processes.

The erosion of trust can be attributed to various factors, including misinformation, political polarization, and perceived failures in crisis management. To restore confidence, transparent and effective communication is essential. Governments and institutions must prioritize clear and timely information sharing, providing accurate updates on the status of the pandemic, vaccination efforts, and public health measures. This can be seen in the successful example of New Zealand, where Prime Minister Jacinda Ardern's regular and transparent communication during the pandemic contributed to high levels of public trust and compliance.

Technology plays a vital role in fostering transparency and accountability. Digital platforms and data-driven approaches can enhance governance by facilitating access to information and enabling citizen engagement. For instance, in South Korea, the "Corona 100m" app provided real-time updates on COVID-19 cases and testing locations, empowering citizens with transparent and accessible data. Similarly, the Open Government Partnership (OGP), an international initiative, promotes the use of technology to strengthen transparency, accountability, and citizen participation in governance processes.

Civil society organizations, media, and whistleblowing mechanisms also play a crucial role in holding institutions accountable. These actors act as watchdogs, exposing wrongdoing and advocating for transparency and ethical practices. One notable example is the International Consortium of Investigative Journalists (ICIJ), which exposed the "Panama Papers" leak, revealing global tax evasion and money laundering schemes. Such investigative journalism efforts shed light on corruption and illicit practices, fostering public scrutiny and pushing for greater accountability.

Promoting inclusivity and involving diverse stakeholders in decision-making processes is essential for rebuilding trust.

By prioritizing the voices of marginalized communities and incorporating their perspectives, policies and actions can address the needs and concerns of all members of society. The Participatory Budgeting initiative in Porto Alegre, Brazil, is an exemplary case of inclusive decision-making. Through this process, citizens directly engage in determining budget allocations, promoting transparency, and empowering communities to shape their destinies.

Accountability mechanisms, anti-corruption measures, and ethical practices are vital for restoring trust in institutions. The establishment of independent oversight bodies, such as ombudsman offices or anti-corruption commissions, can ensure that institutions are held accountable for their actions. For instance, the Integrity Pacts, a tool developed by Transparency International, promote transparency and integrity in public procurement processes, reducing corruption risks.

In conclusion, rebuilding trust in institutions is crucial for the resilience and prosperity of the post-pandemic society. By fostering transparency, strengthening accountability, and prioritizing inclusive decision-making, we can restore confidence in government and institutions. Real-world examples, such as New Zealand's transparent communication, the use of technology in South Korea, investigative journalism efforts by the ICIJ, and participatory budgeting in Brazil, demonstrate the transformative potential of transparency, accountability, and citizen engagement. Together, we can build a society where trust thrives, institutions serve the public interest, and the foundations of democracy are strengthened.

CHAPTER 12: EMBRACING THE POWER OF COLLABORATION: THE STRENGTH OF GLOBAL COOPERATION AND OVERCOMING CHALLENGES TOGETHER

The COVID-19 pandemic has underscored the importance of collaboration and global cooperation in addressing shared challenges. In this chapter, we will explore the significance of interdisciplinary collaboration, public-private partnerships, and community-level cooperation in building a resilient post-pandemic society.

Interdisciplinary collaboration brings together individuals from diverse fields, fostering innovation and collective intelligence. By exchanging ideas and expertise, professionals from different backgrounds can tackle complex problems more effectively. For example, the collaboration between scientists, medical professionals, and engineers has led to the rapid development of diagnostic tests, therapeutics, and vaccines during the pandemic. This interdisciplinary approach harnesses the power of diverse perspectives to drive impactful solutions.

Public-private partnerships have also played a vital role in addressing societal challenges. By leveraging the resources, expertise, and innovation of both sectors, sustainable solutions that benefit society can be created. One notable example is the Access to COVID-19 Tools (ACT) Accelerator, a global collaboration that brings together governments, philanthropic organizations, and pharmaceutical companies to ensure equitable access to COVID-19 tests, treatments, and vaccines. Such partnerships leverage the strengths of each sector to maximize impact and drive positive change.

At the community level, collaboration is crucial for addressing local challenges, building resilience, and fostering social cohesion. Grassroots initiatives, community engagement, and collective action can empower communities to find context-specific solutions. For instance, community-led projects focused on renewable energy, waste management, or education can address local needs while fostering a sense of ownership and unity.

The post-pandemic society presents us with a range of global challenges that demand collaboration and cooperation. Climate change, economic disparities, and peace and security issues require collective action. Collaborative efforts, such as international agreements like the Paris Agreement on climate change, exemplify the strength of global cooperation in addressing shared challenges. By working together, nations can pool resources, share best practices, and drive sustainable development for the benefit of present and future generations.

Embracing the Power of Collaboration invites readers to recognize the transformative potential of collaboration. By embracing interdisciplinary collaboration, public-private partnerships, and community-level cooperation, we can overcome challenges and build a post-pandemic society that is more inclusive, resilient, and sustainable. Real-life examples, such as the interdisciplinary efforts in scientific research and vaccine development, the ACT Accelerator partnership, and community-led initiatives, demonstrate the power of collaboration in driving positive change. Together, we can harness the strength of global cooperation and create a brighter future for all.

The COVID-19 pandemic has disrupted traditional education systems and highlighted the importance of adapting to meet the needs of the future. In this chapter, we will explore the lessons learned from the pandemic and how they can inform the transformation of education.

One key aspect is the role of technology in enhancing learning experiences. The pandemic has accelerated the adoption of online learning platforms, virtual classrooms, and digital resources. For example, platforms like Khan Academy and Coursera provide access to a wide range of educational content. These technological advancements have the potential to create more personalized and interactive learning environments, catering to the diverse needs of students.

Another crucial aspect is the development of new teaching methodologies. The pandemic has prompted educators to explore innovative approaches to engage students in remote and hybrid learning settings. This includes project-based learning, gamification, and collaborative online activities. By embracing these methodologies, educators can foster critical thinking, creativity, problem-solving, and adaptability among students.

Addressing the digital divide is paramount in ensuring equitable access to education. The pandemic has highlighted the disparities in access to technology and internet connectivity among students. Efforts should be made to bridge this divide by providing devices, internet access, and digital literacy training to underserved communities. For example, initiatives like One Laptop per Child and Internet.org aim to provide affordable access to technology and online resources for students worldwide.

In addition to traditional education models, non-traditional approaches such as vocational training, apprenticeships, and online platforms have gained prominence. These alternative pathways can prepare individuals for the rapidly evolving job market by equipping them with practical skills and industry-relevant knowledge. Organizations like Udacity and LinkedIn Learning offer online courses and certifications in various fields, enabling individuals to upskill and reskill according to market demands.

A more flexible and interdisciplinary approach to education is necessary for the post-pandemic society. The pandemic has highlighted the importance of adaptability and resilience. By fostering critical thinking, creativity, and problem-solving skills, education can empower individuals to navigate uncertain and complex situations. Emphasizing interdisciplinary learning encourages students to make connections across different subjects and develop a holistic understanding of the world.

Furthermore, education should embrace lifelong learning as a mindset. In a rapidly changing world, continuous learning is essential for personal and professional growth. Cultivating a culture of curiosity, self-directed learning, and embracing new challenges is crucial. Lifelong learning can be facilitated through online platforms, professional development programs, and community-based learning initiatives.

Emerging technologies such as artificial intelligence and virtual reality hold great potential in enhancing lifelong learning experiences. AI-powered adaptive learning platforms can personalize learning journeys, tailoring content and resources to individual needs and preferences. Virtual reality simulations can create immersive and interactive learning environments, providing practical experiences in various fields.

Education and Skills for the Future call for a transformation in education systems that is adaptable, inclusive, and lifelong. By leveraging technology, embracing new teaching methodologies, addressing the digital divide, promoting interdisciplinary learning, and fostering a culture of lifelong learning, education can equip individuals with the skills and knowledge needed to thrive in the post-pandemic society. Real-life examples, such as online learning platforms, vocational training initiatives, and the use of emerging technologies, demonstrate the potential for innovation and progress in education.

CHAPTER 14: A GREENER AND SUSTAINABLE FUTURE: ENVIRONMENTAL CONSCIOUSNESS, CLIMATE ACTION, AND INVESTING IN SUSTAINABLE SOLUTIONS

The COVID-19 pandemic has brought into sharp focus the urgent need to address environmental issues and take decisive action to combat climate change. In this chapter, we will explore the role of individuals, communities, businesses, and governments in creating a greener and more sustainable future.

Environmental consciousness is vital in fostering a collective commitment to protect our planet. The impact of human activities on the environment, such as deforestation, pollution, and greenhouse gas emissions, has become increasingly evident.

Real-life examples showcase the consequences of these activities and the need for sustainable practices to mitigate their effects.

For instance, the deforestation of the Amazon rainforest has not only led to the loss of valuable biodiversity but also contributed to increased carbon dioxide emissions. Efforts to address this issue include the Amazon Rainforest Fund, founded by Leonardo DiCaprio, which supports indigenous communities and environmental organizations working towards forest preservation.

The importance of preserving biodiversity, ensuring clean air and water, and promoting sustainable food systems cannot be overstated. One example is the United Nations' Sustainable Development Goal 14, which aims to conserve and sustainably use the oceans, seas, and marine resources. Initiatives like the Ocean Clean-up, led by Boyan Slat, focus on removing plastic waste from the world's oceans to protect marine life and ecosystems.

Nature-based solutions and eco-friendly technologies offer promising ways to address environmental challenges. The Great Green Wall project in Africa is an excellent example. This initiative aims to combat desertification by planting a green belt across the Sahel region. By restoring vegetation cover, the project prevents soil erosion, conserves water resources, and promotes biodiversity.

The financial sector plays a pivotal role in driving sustainability through sustainable finance and impact investing. For instance, the Green Bond market has witnessed significant growth, with companies and governments issuing bonds to finance environmentally friendly projects. An example is Apple's Green Bond issuance, where proceeds were allocated to renewable energy projects and energy-efficient buildings.

Corporate social responsibility (CSR) practices are essential in achieving sustainability goals. Companies like Patagonia have become leaders in environmental stewardship. They have implemented sustainable supply chains, embraced circular economy principles, and donated a portion of their profits to environmental causes. Unilever is another notable example, with its Sustainable Living Plan that focuses on reducing environmental impact and improving social conditions.

To inspire and motivate action, real-life examples of sustainable initiatives and organizations serve as beacons of change. The Rocky Mountain Institute, a non-profit organization, works to accelerate the transition to a clean energy future. Their projects include the adoption of renewable energy in Caribbean islands and the promotion of energy-efficient building practices worldwide.

The potential of renewable energy, energy efficiency measures, sustainable transportation solutions, and effective waste management systems cannot be overlooked. Countries like Denmark have made significant progress in renewable energy adoption, with wind energy accounting for a substantial portion of their electricity generation. Electric vehicle manufacturers, such as Tesla, are paving the way for sustainable transportation by popularizing electric cars and investing in charging infrastructure.

A Greener and Sustainable Future calls for collective action and commitment to protect our planet. By fostering environmental consciousness, embracing sustainable practices, and investing in innovative solutions, we can create a post-pandemic society that is environmentally resilient, socially equitable, and economically prosperous. Real-life examples of sustainable initiatives and the potential of nature-based solutions and eco-friendly technologies serve as inspirations for individuals, communities, businesses, and governments to take decisive action towards a greener future.

CHAPTER 15: NEW NORMS IN SOCIAL INTERACTIONS: REDEFINING SOCIAL ETIQUETTE AND NAVIGATING PERSONAL RELATIONSHIPS

The COVID-19 pandemic has profoundly reshaped the way we interact with one another. In this chapter, we will explore the new norms in social interactions and the redefinition of social etiquette in post-pandemic society.

One of the significant changes in social interactions is the alteration of physical greetings and gestures. Handshakes and hugs, once common expressions of warmth and connection, have given way to alternative forms of greeting that prioritize safety and personal space. For example, the "elbow bump" or the "foot shake" has emerged as a contactless way to greet others.

The pandemic has also highlighted the importance of wearing

masks, practising proper hygiene, and maintaining physical distancing as essential elements of responsible social behaviour. These measures have become integral to preventing the spread of the virus and protecting the health of individuals and communities. Real-life examples include the widespread adoption of mask-wearing in public spaces and the use of hand sanitisers in social gatherings.

Technology has played a crucial role in shaping social interactions during the pandemic. The rise of virtual communication platforms, such as video conferencing apps and social media, has enabled people to stay connected while maintaining physical distance. Virtual meetings, online socializing, and remote collaboration have become the new normal for both personal and professional interactions. For instance, platforms like Zoom, Microsoft Teams, and FaceTime have facilitated virtual gatherings, allowing people to celebrate birthdays, weddings, and other significant events from the safety of their homes.

While virtual interactions offer advantages, they also present challenges. Effective communication and digital literacy have become essential skills in this new era. Non-verbal cues and body language may be harder to interpret through a screen, requiring individuals to adapt their communication styles. Real-life examples include the need for clear and concise virtual presentations, active listening in video conferences, and utilizing virtual tools effectively to facilitate collaboration.

Personal relationships have also undergone significant adjustments during the pandemic. Individuals have found creative ways to maintain connections with loved ones while adhering to safety guidelines. Virtual game nights, online movie watch parties, and virtual book clubs have emerged as innovative ways to foster shared experiences. Emotional support, empathy, and understanding have become even more critical in navigating the emotional toll of the pandemic on personal relationships.

Long-distance relationships have faced unique challenges during this time. The importance of effective communication and the role of technology in fostering and maintaining connections have become evident. Real-life examples include couples using video calls to bridge the distance, families organizing virtual reunions to stay connected, and friends planning online gatherings to maintain their bond.

Finding a balance between virtual and in-person interactions has become a delicate task for families, couples, and friends. Everyone has different comfort levels and risk factors to consider. Some may choose to have socially distanced meetups in outdoor settings, while others may opt for entirely virtual interactions. Respect for personal choices and open communication have become crucial elements in maintaining strong relationships.

The pandemic has also brought to light the issue of social isolation and its implications for mental health and well-being. Many individuals have experienced feelings of loneliness and disconnection due to physical distancing measures. Strategies for combating loneliness include fostering social connections through online communities, joining interest-based virtual groups, and participating in local community initiatives. Real-life examples include online support groups, virtual fitness classes, and community volunteer programs.

New Norms in Social Interactions encourages readers to navigate the complexities of social interactions with empathy, understanding, and a commitment to public health. It emphasizes the importance of adapting to the evolving social landscape while maintaining meaningful connections and preserving the fabric of society. By embracing the new norms and finding innovative ways to stay connected, we can foster a sense of belonging and strengthen personal relationships in the post-pandemic era.

CHAPTER 16: THE POWER OF RESILIENCE AND HOPE: LESSONS FROM THE PANDEMIC AND BUILDING A BRIGHTER FUTURE

The COVID-19 pandemic has tested the resilience of individuals, communities, and societies worldwide. In this chapter, we reflect on the profound lessons we have learned from this unprecedented global crisis and explore how we can harness the power of resilience and hope to shape a brighter future in the post-pandemic society.

The pandemic has forced us to adapt and find innovative solutions in the face of adversity. Real-life examples abound, showcasing individuals and communities that have demonstrated remarkable resilience. For instance, healthcare workers who tirelessly cared for the sick, scientists who collaborated across borders to develop vaccines, and community organizations that mobilized resources to support vulnerable populations. These stories of perseverance and determination serve as inspiration, reminding us of the human spirit's capacity to overcome challenges.

Empathy and compassion have also emerged as critical values during this crisis. The pandemic has revealed the interconnectedness of our world, highlighting the importance of supporting one another. Communities have come together, with acts of kindness, solidarity, and community support taking centre stage. From neighbours checking in on each other to organizations providing food and supplies to those in need, these examples demonstrate the power of human connection and the potential for positive change when we stand together.

Investing in healthcare systems and disaster preparedness has become paramount in preventing and mitigating future crises. The lessons learned from the pandemic emphasize the need for robust healthcare infrastructure, early detection systems, and effective crisis response mechanisms. Real-life examples such as the establishment of dedicated infectious disease centres, the expansion of healthcare facilities, and the development of rapid testing capabilities demonstrate the importance of proactive measures in safeguarding public health.

Technology and innovation have played a pivotal role in driving economic recovery and creating new employment opportunities. Remote work, e-commerce, and digital platforms have surged, transforming industries, and opening new possibilities. Companies that embraced digital transformation quickly adapted their operations, while start-ups and entrepreneurs seized the opportunity to innovate in areas such as telehealth, contactless delivery services, and online education. These examples illustrate the resilience and adaptability of individuals and businesses in the face of disruption.

Inclusive policies are crucial for building a brighter future. The pandemic has exposed and exacerbated existing inequalities, underscoring the need for policies that address social justice, environmental sustainability, and economic disparities. Real-life examples of inclusive policies include measures to ensure equitable vaccine distribution, initiatives to promote affordable housing and accessible healthcare, and policies that support renewable energy and environmental conservation. These actions reflect a commitment to creating a society that leaves no one behind.

Maintaining hope and optimism is essential as we navigate the challenges of rebuilding and transformation. Psychological research and practical techniques provide valuable insights for cultivating resilience and fostering a positive mindset. Real-life examples demonstrate the power of hope in action, from individuals who have overcome personal hardships to communities that have risen from the ashes to rebuild and thrive. These stories inspire us to embrace optimism, find meaning in adversity, and work collectively towards a brighter future.

The Power of Resilience and Hope serves as a guiding light, reminding us that even in the face of adversity, we can rise above challenges and build a better future. By harnessing the lessons learned from the pandemic, fostering empathy and compassion, investing in healthcare and technology, implementing inclusive policies, and cultivating hope, we can shape a post-pandemic society that is more resilient, equitable, sustainable, and filled with hope for generations to come.

CHAPTER 17: THE ROLE OF LEADERSHIP IN THE NEW NORMAL: LEADERSHIP IN TIMES OF CRISIS AND INSPIRING CHANGE AND TRANSFORMATION

Effective leadership plays a pivotal role in times of crisis, and the COVID-19 pandemic has highlighted the significance of strong and visionary leaders. In this chapter, we delve into the qualities and strategies that define exceptional leadership during challenging times, examining real-world examples, and providing valuable insights for current and aspiring leaders who wish to make a positive impact in their organizations, communities, and beyond.

During the pandemic, leaders have faced the daunting task of navigating the complexities of the crisis, making critical decisions to protect public health, manage resources, and inspire confidence. Leaders who demonstrated clear communication, empathy, and transparency were able to build trust and foster a sense of unity among individuals and communities. For example, New Zealand's Prime Minister, Jacinda Ardern, garnered global acclaim for her empathetic leadership style and effective communication, which instilled a sense of reassurance and unity among the nation's citizens.

Inclusive leadership has also emerged as a key aspect of effective leadership in the post-pandemic society. Leaders who embrace inclusivity prioritize diversity and equity, creating an environment that values different perspectives, encourages collaboration, and champions social justice. One notable example is Microsoft CEO Satya Nadella, who has prioritized diversity and inclusion within the organization, leading to a more inclusive work culture and driving innovation through a variety of perspectives.

Visionary leadership is another crucial attribute for leaders in times of crisis. Visionary leaders set ambitious goals, challenge the status quo, and foster a culture of innovation. Elon Musk, the CEO of Tesla, and SpaceX, exemplifies visionary leadership by pushing the boundaries of technology and sustainable energy, inspiring change, and transformation not only within his companies but also in the broader industry.

Adaptive leadership is equally essential in an ever-evolving world. Leaders who can respond quickly to changing circumstances and embrace new ways of thinking and doing are crucial in the post-pandemic era. Angela Merkel, the Chancellor of Germany, demonstrated adaptive leadership by effectively managing the evolving challenges of the pandemic, implementing timely policy measures, and adapting strategies to mitigate the impact of the crisis.

The role of leadership in the new normal extends beyond crisis management. It encompasses inspiring change and transformation, leading organizations, and communities towards a brighter future. Real-world examples of transformative leaders include Malala Yousafzai, the Nobel laureate and education activist, who advocates for girls' education and social equality, and Tim Cook, the CEO of Apple, who spearheaded the company's transition to focus on sustainability and renewable energy.

In conclusion, effective leadership is paramount in times of crisis, and the COVID-19 pandemic has emphasized the importance of strong and visionary leaders. Clear communication, empathy, inclusivity, adaptability, and a vision for change are crucial qualities for leaders to inspire confidence, foster unity, and drive transformation. Real-world examples of exceptional leaders provide valuable insights and guidance for current and aspiring leaders seeking to navigate challenges, make a positive impact, and shape a brighter future in the post-pandemic society. By embodying these leadership qualities and strategies, individuals can become catalysts for change, driving progress and resilience in their respective fields and communities.

CHAPTER 18: ETHICS AND VALUES IN THE POST-PANDEMIC SOCIETY: REDEFINING ETHICS AND MORALITY AND SHAPING A VALUES-DRIVEN SOCIETY

The COVID-19 pandemic has not only disrupted our lives but has also challenged our ethical and moral frameworks. In this chapter, we delve into the importance of redefining ethics and morality in the post-pandemic society and shaping a values-driven society that promotes fairness, justice, and sustainability.

The pandemic has presented numerous ethical dilemmas that have forced individuals, communities, and societies to confront difficult choices. One such dilemma is the allocation of limited resources, such as medical supplies and equipment, where ethical considerations of fairness and utility come into play. Real-world examples, such as the triage protocols implemented in overwhelmed hospitals, highlight the challenging decisions healthcare professionals have had to make to save as many lives as possible. These experiences prompt us to reflect on the principles that guide resource allocation and the need for collective re-evaluation of our ethical frameworks.

Another ethical dilemma arises in the context of vaccine distribution. The global demand for vaccines has sparked debates about equitable access and fairness. Real-world examples, such as the COVAX initiative, which aims to ensure fair and equitable distribution of vaccines to low-income countries, demonstrate the importance of international cooperation and solidarity in addressing these ethical challenges. These examples highlight the ethical imperative of prioritizing the health and well-being of all individuals, regardless of their socioeconomic status or geographic location.

The pandemic has also raised questions about balancing personal freedoms and public health. Governments have implemented measures such as lockdowns and social distancing to mitigate the spread of the virus, but these measures have often restricted individual freedoms. Real-world examples of countries implementing strict lockdowns, such as New Zealand and Australia, demonstrate how these measures can effectively control the virus but also raise ethical considerations regarding individual liberties. These examples underscore the delicate balance between safeguarding public health and respecting individual rights, requiring careful ethical deliberation.

Compassion plays a crucial role in ethical decision-making, particularly in times of crisis. The pandemic has highlighted the importance of considering the well-being of others and making choices that prioritize the greater good. Real-world examples of individuals and communities coming together to support vulnerable populations, such as volunteering efforts to deliver groceries to the elderly or organizing mutual aid networks, exemplify the power of compassion in driving ethical actions. These examples emphasize the significance of empathy, understanding, and collective responsibility in shaping a values-driven society.

To cultivate ethical values in the post-pandemic society, education and awareness play a vital role. By incorporating ethics education into school curricula and promoting dialogue on ethical issues, we can instil values such as integrity, respect, and empathy in future generations. Real-world examples of schools and universities integrating ethics into their programs and offering courses on ethics and moral reasoning demonstrate the commitment to shaping the ethical leaders of tomorrow. These initiatives lay the foundation for a society grounded in ethical principles and values.

The post-pandemic society offers us an opportunity to redefine ethics and morality. By addressing the concepts of ethics and values, we aim to inspire reflection and action. Through real-world examples, we see the complexities of ethical decision-making and the importance of compassion in driving ethical behaviour. This chapter encourages readers to consider the ethical implications of their choices and actively participate in shaping a society that is guided by shared values and principles. By fostering a values-driven society, we can collectively work towards a fair, just, and sustainable future.

An awareness of the concepts of ethics and values in the post-pandemic society will serve to inspire reflection and action. It aims to encourage individuals to consider the ethical implications of their choices and to actively participate in shaping a society that is guided by shared values and principles.

CHAPTER 19: INNOVATIONS AND DISCOVERIES IN SCIENCE AND MEDICINE: BREAKTHROUGHS IN MEDICAL RESEARCH AND HARNESSING TECHNOLOGY FOR HEALTHCARE ADVANCEMENTS

The COVID-19 pandemic has sparked a wave of innovation and scientific breakthroughs in the field of medicine. In this chapter, we will explore the remarkable advancements that have emerged and their potential to shape the future of healthcare in the post-pandemic society.

One of the most significant developments in the fight against COVID-19 has been the rapid development and deployment of vaccines. Scientists, researchers, and pharmaceutical companies around the world have collaborated to develop safe and effective vaccines in record time. Examples include the mRNA vaccines developed by Pfizer-BioNTech and Moderna, which have demonstrated high efficacy rates in preventing COVID-19. These breakthroughs highlight the power of scientific collaboration and the potential for revolutionary vaccine development strategies in the future.

Beyond COVID-19, there have been notable discoveries and advancements in medical research during this time. Gene therapy, for instance, has shown promise in treating genetic disorders by replacing or repairing faulty genes. Regenerative medicine, including stem cell therapies, holds the potential for tissue repair and organ transplantation. Diagnostic tools have also seen advancements, with the development of innovative technologies for early disease detection and monitoring. Additionally, personalized medicine has gained traction, tailoring treatments to an individual's genetic makeup and lifestyle factors.

The rise of telemedicine has transformed healthcare access and delivery. Remote consultations allow patients to receive medical advice and prescriptions from the comfort of their homes, reducing the need for in-person visits. Artificial intelligence (AI) and machine learning algorithms are being integrated into healthcare systems to support diagnosis and treatment decisions. AI can analyse vast amounts of medical data and provide insights to healthcare professionals, enabling more accurate and timely interventions.

One crucial aspect that deserves attention is the holistic approach to healthcare. While medical advancements are vital, it is equally important to consider the emotional, psychological, and social well-being of patients. The integration of holistic practices, such as mindfulness, patient-centred care, and mental health support, can enhance overall patient outcomes and satisfaction.

Digital health technologies have also revolutionized public health monitoring and management. Wearable devices, such as smartwatches and fitness trackers, enable individuals to track their health metrics and detect early signs of potential health issues. Health apps provide tools for self-monitoring, medication reminders, and accessing medical information. Data analytics allow for real-time tracking of disease outbreaks and population health trends, facilitating proactive interventions.

However, the adoption of technology in healthcare raises ethical considerations. Ensuring data privacy and security is crucial to protect patients' sensitive information. Striking a balance between technological advancements and preserving the human touch in healthcare is essential to maintain the quality of patient care and establish trust.

Real-life examples illustrate the impact of these innovations. For instance, the use of telemedicine has surged during the pandemic, allowing healthcare professionals to remotely diagnose and treat patients. Wearable devices have played a role in monitoring COVID-19 symptoms and facilitating remote patient monitoring. Additionally, the rapid development of COVID-19 tests using innovative diagnostic technologies has enabled widespread testing and helped control the spread of the virus.

In conclusion, the post-pandemic era has witnessed significant advancements in medical research and the integration of technology in healthcare. These breakthroughs hold great promise for improving patient outcomes, expanding access to care, and transforming the way we approach healthcare. However, it is essential to consider the holistic well-being of individuals and address ethical considerations to ensure that these advancements benefit all and contribute to a healthier and more resilient society in the future.

CHAPTER 20: THE NEW LANDSCAPE OF GOVERNANCE: RESHAPING POLITICAL SYSTEMS AND REINVENTING POLICY-MAKING PROCESSES

The COVID-19 pandemic has brought significant changes to governance systems across the globe. In this chapter, we delve into the transformative effects of the crisis on political systems and explore how governments have responded to the challenges presented by the pandemic.

The pandemic has underscored the critical role of leadership in times of crisis and the importance of transparent and effective governance. Governments have faced the unprecedented task of addressing the public health crisis, managing the economic impacts, and restoring societal confidence. Real-life examples abound of leaders who have demonstrated exemplary crisis management skills, providing clear communication, making difficult decisions, and implementing policies to protect public health and well-being. For instance, New Zealand's Prime Minister Jacinda Ardern garnered international recognition for her empathetic and decisive leadership, implementing strict measures that effectively contained the spread of the virus within the country.

Adaptive governance has emerged as a key concept in navigating the complexities of the pandemic. It emphasizes the need for flexibility and responsiveness in policymaking. Governments have been compelled to adapt their decision-making processes and policies to the rapidly evolving circumstances of the pandemic. This includes regularly reviewing and updating guidelines based on emerging scientific evidence and adjusting measures to balance public health concerns with socioeconomic impacts. Singapore's approach to governance during the pandemic serves as an example, with the government implementing a nuanced and data-driven strategy that includes targeted testing, contact tracing, and public communication campaigns to manage the spread of the virus while minimizing disruptions to the economy.

Data-driven policymaking has played a crucial role in informing government decisions during the pandemic. The use of scientific expertise and analysis of real-time data has helped guide policy formulation and implementation. Governments have relied on insights from epidemiologists, virologists, and public health experts to develop evidence-based strategies. For instance, South Korea's successful containment of the virus was attributed, in part, to its extensive testing and contact tracing efforts, which were supported by a robust public health infrastructure and the use of advanced technology for rapid data analysis.

Effective governance in the post-pandemic society requires a balance between expertise-driven decision-making and meaningful stakeholder engagement. Governments have increasingly turned to digital platforms to facilitate public consultations, citizen engagement, and feedback mechanisms.

Examples include virtual town hall meetings, online surveys, and social media platforms, which have allowed for broader participation and inclusive policymaking. The Estonian government's digital governance initiatives have been noteworthy, leveraging e-governance platforms to ensure transparency, efficiency, and citizen involvement in policy development and decision-making processes.

Policy resilience has emerged as a crucial aspect of governance in the face of future crises. Governments are recognizing the need to build robust and adaptable policy frameworks that can withstand unforeseen challenges. Lessons learned from the pandemic, such as the importance of early intervention, preparedness, and cooperation between governments and international organizations, can inform the development of more resilient governance systems. For instance, the African Union's Africa CDC initiative has demonstrated the importance of regional collaboration and coordination in responding to public health emergencies, leading to strengthened healthcare systems and improved crisis response capabilities across the continent.

The new landscape of governance in the post-pandemic society necessitates the reinvention of policy-making processes to effectively address the multifaceted challenges ahead. Governments must adapt to the changing needs and expectations of their citizens, harness technology for more inclusive and transparent governance, and foster collaboration and innovation. By embracing these transformative approaches, governments can build resilient, responsive, and inclusive societies that are better equipped to navigate future crises and promote the well-being of their populations.

CHAPTER 21: MENTAL HEALTH AND EMOTIONAL WELL-BEING: ADDRESSING THE PSYCHOLOGICAL IMPACT OF THE PANDEMIC AND PROMOTING EMOTIONAL RESILIENCE

The COVID-19 pandemic has had far-reaching implications for our mental health and emotional well-being, significantly impacting individuals and communities worldwide. In this chapter, we delve into the psychological consequences of the pandemic and discuss strategies for addressing and mitigating its effects in the post-pandemic society.

The pandemic has brought about a surge in mental health challenges, including increased levels of anxiety, depression, and stress. Individuals have faced various factors contributing to these challenges, such as social isolation, fear of infection, and economic uncertainties. Frontline workers, caregivers, and vulnerable populations have experienced unique psychological burdens due to their roles and circumstances.

To create a society that supports mental health, it is crucial to de-stigmatize mental health issues and foster a culture of open dialogue and support. By encouraging conversations around mental health and promoting awareness, we can help individuals feel comfortable seeking help and accessing necessary resources. Mental health professionals, community organizations, and government initiatives play a vital role in providing accessible and effective mental health services to those in need. Furthermore, teletherapy and digital mental health platforms have emerged as valuable tools for extending mental health support to remote areas and underserved communities.

Promoting emotional resilience is essential in the post-pandemic society as individuals navigate through ongoing challenges. Strategies and tools exist to help individuals build emotional resilience and adapt to the new normal. Self-care practices, such as mindfulness, meditation, and regular exercise, are effective in managing stress and enhancing emotional well-being. Maintaining healthy relationships and social connections play a significant role in fostering emotional resilience and providing support during difficult times. Education and awareness play a crucial role in promoting emotional intelligence and equipping individuals with the skills to navigate difficult emotions and situations. Emotional intelligence training in schools, workplaces, and community settings can greatly contribute to the overall well-being of individuals and communities.

Addressing mental health and emotional well-being requires

a comprehensive approach. Early intervention, prevention programs, and ongoing support systems are vital in ensuring individuals have the resources they need to thrive mentally and emotionally. By prioritizing mental health services, implementing preventive measures, and promoting emotional well-being, we can create a society that values and supports the mental well-being of its members.

Real-life examples of initiatives and programs that have successfully addressed mental health challenges during the pandemic can serve as inspiration. For instance, organizations have developed online mental health resources and support groups to reach individuals who may not have access to traditional services. Schools have implemented emotional intelligence curricula and integrated mental health support into their programs. Governments have launched campaigns to raise awareness, reduce stigma, and expand mental health services in their communities.

In conclusion, the psychological impact of the COVID-19 pandemic cannot be overlooked. By addressing mental health challenges, promoting emotional resilience, and prioritizing emotional well-being, we can create a society that values and supports the mental health of its members. Let us embark on this journey of healing and resilience, working together to build a post-pandemic society that fosters emotional well-being for all.

The COVID-19 pandemic has tested the resilience and adaptability of individuals and communities across the globe. In this chapter, we explore the valuable lessons learned from the post-pandemic society and discuss the possibilities for a brighter future.

One significant lesson from the pandemic is the power of unity, compassion, and collective action. Despite the hardships faced, we have witnessed inspiring stories of resilience that demonstrate the indomitable human spirit. Acts of kindness, innovation, and collaboration have emerged as individuals and communities come together to support one another. From grassroots initiatives delivering essential supplies to frontline workers to virtual platforms connecting people worldwide, these examples remind us of the strength and potential of human connection.

Preparedness and proactive measures are crucial in mitigating the impact of future crises. The pandemic has highlighted the importance of robust healthcare systems, effective communication strategies, and global cooperation in managing and preventing outbreaks. Investing in healthcare infrastructure, advancing medical research, and implementing early warning systems are key elements in building resilience for the future. By learning from this crisis, we can be better prepared to respond to emerging challenges and protect the well-being of individuals and societies.

Looking ahead, the post-pandemic society presents opportunities for positive social and environmental changes. It calls for a re-evaluation of our priorities and lifestyles, embracing sustainable practices and technology. We have witnessed the positive impacts of reduced carbon emissions during lockdowns, the revitalization of local communities, and a renewed appreciation for nature. By harnessing these lessons, we can work towards creating a more equitable, resilient, and environmentally conscious world.

Continued learning and adaptation are essential in navigating future uncertainties. The post-pandemic society calls for ongoing innovation, agility, and a growth mindset. Education, research, and lifelong learning play pivotal roles in equipping individuals and societies with the tools to thrive in a rapidly changing world. By embracing new knowledge, fostering creativity, and embracing emerging technologies, we can overcome challenges and seize opportunities for progress.

Optimism, hope, and forward-thinking are essential in shaping a brighter future. The lessons learned from the post-pandemic society serve as a foundation for building a better world.

It is crucial to prioritize human connection, well-being, and sustainability in our collective endeavours. By nurturing a sense of optimism and hope, we can inspire and mobilize individuals and communities to work towards a future that is inclusive, compassionate, and environmentally conscious.

Real-life examples of transformative initiatives emerging from the post-pandemic society serve as beacons of hope. For instance, community-led projects focused on sustainable agriculture, renewable energy, and social justice have gained momentum. Businesses are adopting environmentally friendly practices and investing in social impact initiatives. Governments are implementing policies that prioritize public health, equity, and environmental sustainability. These examples illustrate the potential for positive change when individuals and institutions come together with a shared vision for a better world.

In conclusion, the post-pandemic society has taught us invaluable lessons about resilience, compassion, and the importance of preparedness. It is a time to reimagine and shape a brighter future. By embracing sustainable practices, fostering a culture of lifelong learning, and nurturing optimism, we can build a world that is resilient, inclusive, and environmentally conscious. Let us draw upon the wisdom gained from the post-pandemic society and work together towards a future that prioritizes the well-being of individuals, communities, and the planet.

Conclusion:
Embracing the Post-Pandemic Society and
Shaping Our Collective Destiny

In this concluding chapter, we reflect on the journey we have taken through the exploration of the post-pandemic society. We have unmasked the new normal and examined the various aspects that shape our lives and communities in this transformative era. Now, it is time to embrace the post-pandemic society and all the opportunities and challenges it presents.

Throughout this book, we have witnessed the resilience, innovation, and adaptability of individuals, communities, and nations. We have seen how the pandemic has forced us to re-evaluate our priorities, redefine our social interactions, and reimagine the way we work, learn, and connect. It has been a time of reflection, growth, and transformation.

As we move forward into the post-pandemic society, we must remember that we have the power to shape our collective destiny. We have seen the potential for positive change, in building a more inclusive, sustainable, and resilient world. It is up to us to take the lessons learned and translate them into action.

We must prioritize the well-being of individuals and communities, fostering a sense of solidarity, empathy, and compassion. We must continue to invest in education, healthcare, and social support systems that ensure the thriving of all members of society. We must embrace technology and innovation, harnessing their power for positive impact while remaining mindful of the ethical implications.

It is also crucial that we work together on a global scale. The challenges we face transcend borders and require international cooperation and collaboration. We must forge partnerships, share knowledge and resources, and unite in our efforts to address global crises, from climate change to social inequality.

In conclusion, the post-pandemic society is an opportunity for us to rebuild, reimagine, and shape a better future. It is a time to learn from the past, adapt to the present, and envision a more resilient and sustainable world. Let us embrace the new normal with optimism, creativity, and a collective sense of purpose.

As we navigate the complexities and uncertainties of this transformative era, let us remember the lessons learned, the resilience demonstrated, and the connections forged. Together, we can create a post-pandemic society that is characterized by compassion, equity, and the pursuit of a better future for all.

Thank you for embarking on this journey with us, and may our collective efforts pave the way for a brighter and more inclusive post-pandemic society.